Zippo Lighters

FIELD GUIDE

Dana & Robin Baumgartner

Values and Identification

©2006 Krause Publications

Published by

700 East State Street • Iola, WI 54990-0001
715-445-2214 • 888-457-2873

Our toll-free number to place an order or obtain
a free catalog is (800) 258-0929.

Library of Congress Catalog Number: 2005934361
ISBN 13-digit: 978-0-89689-362-7
ISBN 10-digit: 0-89689-362-6
Designed by Donna Mummery
Edited by Kristine Manty

Printed in China

ACKNOWLEDGMENTS

A special thanks to Peggy Sheils for her hospitality and for graciously allowing me to photograph a portion of her outstanding collection. While I was in that part of the States, Rich Albers and Ron Eyerkuss also shared some lighters—thank you. A big thank you to Rolf Gerster who provided us with the vast majority of the military section and respective values. We also appreciate Roger Foley and Len Shorter for their contributions. Our thanks to Ron Chapin and Mike Grimaldi for their support and for shipping their and Michelle Pohl's precious lighters to us for photographing. Ira Pilossof's support and assistance were invaluable to us. Thank you also to Kelly Platko of Roseart. To all the fine folks at Zippo Manufacturing Co. who provided us with information (in particular, Kathy Jones and Pat Grandy, who we depended upon the most) —you are much appreciated.

Due to time constraints, we could not contact many collectors for material for this field guide, but we feel sure we would have been afforded the material if requested. To that end, we are very fortunate to be a part of the Zippo lighter collecting community.

To all of you, we thank you from the bottom of our inserts.

CONTENTS

INTRODUCTION

Welcome to the fascinating and fun world of Zippo lighter collecting! There are tens of thousands of Zippo lighter collectors and five lighter collector clubs in the United States. There are also clubs and collectors as far away as Austria, India, Japan, and South Africa, just to name some. Zippo lighters are truly an internationally known collectible.

Our personal collection began in 1986 by our redeeming cigarette coupons for Zippo lighters featuring tobacco advertising on the lighters' cases. Now, almost 20 years later, our passion for collecting Zippo lighters has taken us to swap meets in various states and as far as Europe. We belong to eight lighter collecting clubs and are blessed with friends from around the world who share the same obsession. Half the fun of collecting Zippo lighters, as in any other leisure pursuit of a fine collectible, is meeting the great folks along the way.

This field guide contains a brief history of Zippo Manufacturing Company, general guidelines for collecting its lighters, some basic rules on dating them, and pictures of nearly 500 Zippo lighters and their estimated values. Several full-size books have been published containing great detail regarding Zippo Manufacturing Company's history and dating of Zippo lighters; however, many mysteries remain today. Knowledge is a collector's best friend, so, throughout this guide, you will see helpful Web site links should you desire more detailed knowledge on Zippo Manufacturing Company and Zippo lighters. The best place to begin is Zippo's official Web site: www.zippo.com.

We believe the intent of any price guide is to provide general guidance of prices of collectibles. After reviewing this field guide, you will easily be able to recognize a "full leather" and know that it is more valuable than a "leather wrap," for instance. The values given in this field guide are for Zippo lighters in excellent to mint condition, regardless of the picture shown, and without packaging. If the lighter is in its original box, it may have a greater value; this is especially true with earlier models. A detailed and/or colorful decoration on the front or both sides of the lighter may also drive the price up. A slim-sized Zippo lighter

A lighter touting sales promotion and costumer appreciation.

with the same decoration(s) normally carries a lesser value. Another consideration would be rare vintage Zippo lighters, limited editions, prototypes and salesman samples that wind up in collections or dresser drawers and are seldom seen again. A few of these appear in this field guide and the values are high. This should not be a deterrent to those beginning to collect, as some of today's currently manufactured Zippo lighters will also eventually wind up in those seldom seen collections and drawers.

Factors personal to collectors, such as their ages, preferences, areas of interest, and geographical locations, also play major roles in a Zippo lighter's worth. We favor lighters that feature advertising of companies in Newark, Ohio (our hometown), so we would certainly pay more for one of those than someone who has never heard of Newark. Major brand names advertised on Zippo lighters, such as Coca Cola, often appeal to a wider range than solely Zippo lighter collectors; therefore, these "cross-collectibles" are in higher demand and valued as such. Simply put, a Zippo lighter is worth exactly what a person is willing to pay for it. Price guides have been published in the past and by the time they reach the bookstore shelves the prices can be obsolete. You will most likely find that true here—as with all collectibles, the market fluctuates.

Volumes could be written on the various series, finishes and styles of Zippo lighters. In 2003, Zippo produced its 400 millionth lighter, at which time the company was producing 45,000 lighters a day! So, while we cannot possibly touch on all of them here, we offer you a small sampling and hope this guide will ignite your curiosity and fuel your passion for collecting the world's greatest windproof lighter.

Now that you're fired up, happy hunting!

Dana and Robin Baumgartner

HISTORY

George Grant Blaisdell was born on June 5, 1895, in Bradford, Pennsylvania. In 1931, at the Bradford Country Club, Mr. Blaisdell met a gentleman who was using a lighter made in Austria. The lighter worked exceptionally well, especially in the wind; however, it required the use of both hands. It intrigued Mr. Blaisdell, who envisioned improving upon the design. The word "Zippo" is a spin-off of the word "zipper." The zipper had recently been patented in a nearby town, and Mr. Blaisdell liked the sound of the word. He established Zippo in October 1932 in Bradford and the first Zippo lighter was produced in January 1933. Mr. Blaisdell's lighter had the lid attached to the body and required the use of only one hand to light it, making it less awkward to use and better looking.

The first Zippo lighters retailed for $1.95 each—a costly investment for most people at that time. But with Mr. Blaisdell's guarantee and marketing strategy, "It works or we fix it for free," folks were more willing to part with that kind of money.

The original patent was applied for on May 17, 1934, and patent number 2032695 was granted on March 3, 1936. The 2517191 patent number was issued on August 1, 1950. The Zippo lighter basically remains the same to this day, with just minor improvements.

In the mid-1930s, Kendall Refining Company placed an order for 500 Zippo lighters. These are believed to be the first company-advertised lighters produced by Zippo and are highly collectible. Decades later, companies continue to use Zippo lighters as an advertising medium.

Zippo Manufacturing Company, Canada, Ltd., was established in Ontario, Canada, in 1949 to negate import duties. The facility closed on July 31, 2002.

In 1954, construction began on new offices at 33 Barbour St. in Bradford, and an open house was held in September 1955. The headquarters remain there today.

Mr. Blaisdell passed away on October 3, 1978. He is remembered not only for inventing the Zippo lighter, a great American icon, but also for his generous and kind spirit. After his passing, his daughters, Mrs. Harriett B. Wick and Mrs. Sarah B. Dorn, inherited the business. Robert Galey was chosen to lead the company. He retired in 1986, and the controller, Michael Schuler, was appointed president and chief executive officer. Today, Mrs. Sarah Dorn and her son, Mr. George B. Duke, own Zippo Manufacturing Company. Gregory W. Booth is president and CEO.

The image of George Blaisdell, creator of the Zippo phenomenon, is emblazoned in this lighter.

This philosophy has been the foundation of the Zippo company.

In 1994, Zippo Manufacturing Company began hosting a yearly "National Zippo Day" celebration. Every other year, an international swap meet is held at the same time. Eight thousand people attended the 2004 swap meet.

The Zippo/Case Visitors Center opened in July 1997. It is a 15,000-square-foot facility that includes a store, museum, and the famous Zippo Repair Clinic, where the Zippo lighter repair process can be viewed through expansive windows.

In the fall of 2002, Zippo obtained trademark registration for the "shape" of the Zippo lighter. This was a major milestone for the company. Zippo lighters are often imitated by inferior replicas, but by obtaining this right, Zippo has legally been able to curtail much counterfeiting.

The Zippo Click Collectors Club was formed in 2002 and debuted at that year's international swap meet. At the Zippo/Case International Swap Meet 2004, a members-only get together was held at the Pennhills Country Club, where 54 years earlier Mr. Blaisdell shot a hole-in-one. At this writing, Zippo Click has 9,000+ members from around the world.

By 2004, Zippo lighters had appeared in thousands of movies, on more than 120 television shows, and on stage about 30 times.

Today, though most products are simply disposable or available with limited warranties, the Zippo lighter still comes with its famous lifetime guarantee, "It works or we fix it for free.™" No one has ever spent a cent on the repair of a Zippo lighter regardless of the lighter's age or condition.

COLLECTING ZIPPO LIGHTERS

The great news is Zippo lighters can turn up anywhere. With more than 400 million produced to date, you're bound to spot them in a variety of places. Garage sales, flea markets, and antiques shops are good places to start. We also wouldn't be surprised if your friends and/or family have a special Zippo lighter tucked away. The Internet is chock full of good on-line shopping, too. Displaying your collection is relatively easy due to small size of the lighters. Later on, we'll talk about lighter collector clubs, which are a haven for buying, trading and selling Zippo lighters.

Our collection consists of approximately 600 pieces. Six hundred may sound like a lot to some people, but there are collectors who have thousands. On the other hand, some collections may consist of five or ten Zippo lighters. It's not necessarily about the number of lighters a person

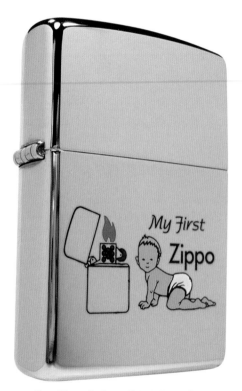

Every Zippo collection needs to start somewhere.

has accumulated in his or her collection—it's the love of these small pieces of art and history or perhaps a piece that strikes a personal feeling that is more important.

Because of the popularity of Zippo lighter collecting, you must be aware of "fakes." Fakes are Zippo lighter look-a-likes, which can sometimes almost fool a seasoned collector. As we already mentioned, Zippo has been granted trademark registration for the shape of the Zippo lighter; however, fakes do continue to slip through the cracks. Indications of fakes are a misspelled advertisement on the front of the case or an incorrect stamping on the bottom of the case (see P. 18 and 19). In the photo on P. 19, you'll see the letter "U" to the left of the word Zippo. The letter should indicate the month of production: A=January through L=December. "U" is an invalid month code. Also, notice the "R" instead of the correct "P" in "Bradford, RA."

Repainted lighters may be nice in your collection, but only if you know they are repainted and don't mind them not being totally original. If the paint is 100 percent but there is brass showing through the chrome plating, for example, the lighter has most likely been repainted (see P. 20 and 21). Zippo Manufacturing Company offers the service of repainting your Zippo lighter for a fee. It should be noted that paint color variances do appear between Zippo lighters manufactured in America and

This copy of a lighter design produced by Zippo is a fake.

The bottom of the lighter, showing the fake manufacturer marks.

those produced in Canada, as well as artwork produced in different years.

The insert—the removable, inner mechanism—often gets exchanged for one reason or another. Distinguishing different model years of inserts is based on the material composition, the verbiage and its position on the insert, the number of holes in the chimney, and numerous other factors. Detailed reference material is a must to correctly identify the exact year of an insert. A good rule of thumb is an insert can possibly be older than the case by a year or so and be the original insert. The flip side is an insert, which is newer than the case, is most likely not the original insert.

The packaging for Zippo lighters has evolved over time. Again, like inserts, your Zippo lighter may be purchased or found in a container that is not original. There is a brief overview in the section "Packaging."

As with any collectible, preserving all original

This lighter still has its original paint.

This one has been repainted.

components increases the value of a piece. If you are looking for an investment, the complete and original packaging, guarantee paperwork, insert and mint case are more important than they might be to a casual collector.

Another lively topic of conversation is whether to remove price and safety stickers from Zippo lighters. Every new Zippo lighter distributed in the U.S. has an orange safety sticker on the back of the case and quite often a price sticker on the front of the case. You'll also find vintage lighters with their original price stickers still intact. So, do you remove the stickers or leave them as is? Welcome to the great sticker debate. These stickers, over time, will cause damage to the lighter's finish. Stickers placed on the lighters by sellers at garage sales or antique shops will do the same damage. The greatest concern is discoloration and glue residue. Discoloration is extremely noticeable on brass finish. If you remove an older sticker, you risk exposing the damage. In our opinion, by removing an older sticker, you are also removing some of the originality of the product. If your lighter has a sticker on it, the lighter is most likely in mint condition; if you remove the sticker and find damage, you will then need to find a method to return the case to its original mint condition, if possible. This, in itself, may cause more damage to the case. High polish chrome is prone to scratching easily. On the other hand, the majority of collectors immediately remove all stickers from recently released lighters, i.e. manufactured within the last 10 years, hoping to prevent damage before it starts. So, do you remove the stickers or leave them as is? We'll leave that sticky decision up to you. Please note we do recommend you immediately remove the flint from any collectible Zippo lighter you currently own or purchase in the future. The flints deteriorate over time and become lodged in the flint tube, which in turn will freeze the flint wheel and can severely damage the tube.

Zippo Manufacturing Company does produce personalized Zippo lighters through its Zippo Promotional Products Division, with a 50-piece minimum order required. The company will take your submitted artwork (some restrictions apply) and create a design of your preference. You may see some of these in your hunting expeditions and we have included several illustrations herein. Fine examples of personalized Zippo lighters are the club lighters shown, and you will see other examples in the Advertising sections.

Joining a lighter collector club is a delightful way to increase your knowledge of Zippo lighters and add to your collection. Many of the clubs publish newsletters, and all of them hold a minimum of one swap meet a year.

Listed here are the five clubs within the United States. Numerous clubs exist throughout the world, and their contact information may be found at the Zippo Click Collectors Club Web site.

Zippo Click Collectors Club

Sponsored by Zippo Manufacturing Company

Web site: www.zippoclick.com

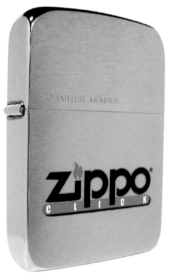

OTLS (On the Lighter Side)
Judith Sanders
Email: info@otls.com
Web site: www.OTLS.com

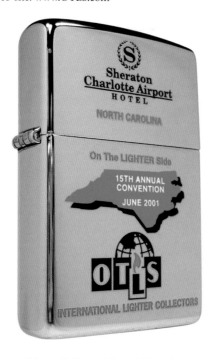

SLLC (Southern Lights Lighter Club)
Bob Whittal
Email: kinziezoo2@cs.com
Web site: www.southernlights.homestead.com

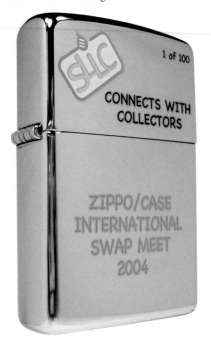

**PLPG (Pocket Lighter
Preservation Guild)**
Larry Marshall
Email: PLPG1@aol.com
Web site:
webpages.charter.net/buylighter

GLLC (Great Lakes Lighter Club)
Len Shorter
Email: LSHO382057@aol.com
Web site:
www.greatlakeslighterclub.homestead.com

DATING ZIPPO LIGHTERS

Mr. Blaisdell had date codes imprinted on the bottom of the lighter cases. These codes provided him with the date of manufacture, should a defect be found, allowing him to maintain records of repairs. Fortunately, those date codes are a tremendous help today in the ability of collectors to correctly identify the year any given Zippo lighter was made. In this guide, we'll discuss only the bottom stampings of the case. Other factors for dating early Zippo lighters are their height and shape, the number of barrels on the hinge and the case's material. Inserts can also be dated by their material, number of holes in the chimney, flint wheel style, cam style, and markings.

Very quickly, you can determine a broad age of a Zippo lighter based on the three major changes to the style of the word "Zippo" imprinted on the bottom of the lighter. The "Block" Zippo was used from 1933 to 1954;

These are various manufacturing marks found on Zippo lighters.

it was changed to the "Script" Zippo in 1955, and the "Flaming i" began in 1980 (see P. 33).

Pat. Pending was stamped from 1933 until the end of 1936, when it was replaced with Pat. 2032695. Pat. 2517191 was stamped from late 1953 until 1967.

Date codes appeared as early as 1955, and the dating system was fully in effect by 1959. Before 1959, dating

Zippo lighters can be a bit tricky, as the exact placement of the words must be taken into consideration. We've provided examples of what we believe to be the correct bottom codes for those tricky years. Again, placement of the wording, the material the case is made of and the number of barrels on the hinge play key factors in dating earlier Zippo lighters.

In 1986, the dot and slash date code methods were replaced with Roman numerals representing the year and letters of the alphabet representing the month of production.

In 2001, the last two digits of the year were used along with the same letters for the months, and that system continues today.

Slim Zippo lighters were introduced in 1956 and had no date code on the bottom of the lighter. Slims were first marked in 1957. From 1957 through 1965, slims had different bottom date codes than did regular size Zippo lighters. Beginning in 1966, the same markings were used on both the slim and regular. In 2002, the holes in the chimney of slim lighters were enlarged.

Dating Zippo lighters produced in Canada from 1950 until 1986 is difficult due to the lack of date coding. The bottom stamps shown here generally provide for time spans.

ZIPPO LIGHTER IDENTIFICATION CODES

YEAR	LEFT	RIGHT

As with most collectibles, the date of manufacture of a Zippo lighter often affects its value. Valuable information on the bottom of every Zippo lighter can help you determine its date of manufacture. Most lighters fabricated between 1933 and 1957 can be identified by style and model and the patent or patent-pending marks.

Starting in the mid 50's date codes were stamped on the bottom. The original purpose was for quality control. The date codes have since become an invaluable tool for Zippo collectors.

The appearance of the word "Zippo" in the bottom stamp provides another clue to dating. There have been three major changes, as shown below.

From 1933 to the mid 50's the word Zippo was stamped in block letters.

ZIPPO

1933	Patent Pending
1937 - c.1950	Patent 2032695
1942 - 1946	Black Crackle, Patent 203695. (This number was stamped in error, should have been Patent 2032695)
c.1950 - c.1957	Patent 2517191
c.1950 - c.1957	Patent 2517191 with patent pending

Zippo records indicate an overlap of bottom stamp configurations from 1949-1957. Also some lighters produced between 1955-57 were date coded, however, specifics remain unclear

The Zippo script logo was developed in the late 40's and was phased-in on the lighter bottom stamp around 1955.

YEAR	LEFT	RIGHT
1958	Patent Pending	
	••••	••••
1959	••••	•••
1960	•••	•••
1961	•••	••
1962	••	••
1963	••	•
1964	•	•
1965	•	
1966	IIII	IIII
1967	IIII	III
1968	III	III
1969	III	II
1970	II	II
1971	II	I
1972	I	
1973	I	
1974	////	////
1975	////	///
1976	///	///
1977	///	//
1978	//	//
1979		

An error was made in the date code. One of the slash marks was removed from the left of the Zippo trademark instead of being removed from the right; thus the code read: / //. This date code error was corrected within the same year to read: // /

In the late 70's the logo was redesigned. It was incorporated into the bottom stamp in 1980.

ZIPPO LIGHTER IDENTIFICATION CODES

YEAR	LEFT	RIGHT
1980	/	/
1981	/	
1982	\\\\	\\\\
1983	\\\\	\\\
1984	\\\	\\\
1985	\\\	\\
1986	\\	\\

Effective July 1, 1986 the dot and slash system was replaced by year / month code. Year is noted with roman numeral; letter designates month (A=Jan., B=Feb., etc.)

1986	G to L	II
1987	A to L	III
1988	A to L	IV
1989	A to L	V
1990	A to L	VI
1991	A to L	VII
1992	A to L	VIII
1993	A to L	IX
1994	A to L	X
1995	A to L	XI

YEAR	LEFT	RIGHT
1996	A to L	XII
1997	A to L	XIII
1998	A to L	XIV
1999	A to L	XV
2000	A to L	XVI

Beginning in 2001, the Roman numerals indicating the year were replaced with numbers corresponding to the last digits of the year of manufacture as follows:

2001	A to L	01
2002	A to L	02
2003	A to L	03
2004	A to L	04
2005	A to L	05
2006	A to L	06
2007	A to L	07
2008	A to L	08
2009	A to L	09
2010	A to L	10

For more collecting information, consult one of several books about Zippo lighters or visit zippoclick.com.

SLIM LIGHTERS

Slim lighters were first introduced in 1956, with a flat bottom and no date code. The first markings were added in 1957 and overlapped into 1958. From 1957-1965 the code configuration on the slim lighters differed from the regular lighters. From 1966 on the configuration has been the same.

1957	••••	••••
1958	••••	••••
	••••	•••
1959	•••	•••
1960	•••	••

1961	••	••
1962	••	•
1963	•	•
1964	•	
1965		

These block letters were used on the bottom of Zippo lighters from 1933 to the mid-1950s.

The 1933-1936 Pat Pending mark.

This is the script logo used circa 1955 to the late 1970s.

The flaming "i" mark used from 1980 to the present.

The Pat 2032695 mark was used from 1936-1940.

Another Pat 2032695 mark used from 1940-1953.

This Pat 2157191, Pat. Pend. mark was used from 1953-1955.

This 1955 mark includes Zippo in script, four dots on the left and right, Pat. 2517191, and Pat. Pend.

This 1956 mark has three dots on the left, four dots on the right, Pat. 2517191, and Pat. Pend.

Four dots on the left and right and Pat. 2517191 make up this 1957 mark. Pat. Pend. has been removed.

This 1958 mark has four dots on the left and right, with Pat. 2517191 centered.

This 1959 mark has three dots on the left, four dots on the right, and Pat. 2517191 centered.

Vertical slashes, with Pat. 2517191 centered, make up this 1966 mark.

The 1974 mark has forward slashes. Pat. 2517191 was removed by 1968.

This 1982 mark has backward slashes.

A 1986 mark has month codes and Roman numerals for years.

Zippo stopped adding Roman numerals to its mark in 2000.

The 2001 mark includes the last two digits of the year.

A Canadian mark from 1949, with Pat. on the left and Pend. on the right.

The Canadian mark used from 1950 to the mid-1960s has Patented on the left and 1950 on the right.

A Canadian mark from the mid-1960s to 1986. Patent information is removed and there is no date coding.

This Canadian mark was used from 1986-2000; shown here is the 1994 version.

This is a Canadian mark from 2001-2002.

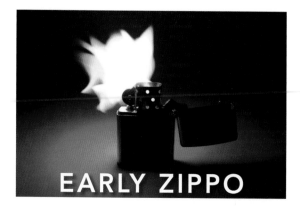

EARLY ZIPPO

The original 1933 lighter was ¼" taller than the Zippo lighter we know today and the case had square corners. The corners were rounded in the late 1930s. The first method used to decorate Zippo lighters was affixing a piece of metal lace, only 5/1000's of an inch thick, to the front of the case using a cement type glue. The so-called "metallique" was then hand painted with enamel paint and baked to set the paint. This process was used from the mid-1930s to the early 1940s.

A 1933 lighter, $10,000+.

A 1934-35 lighter, Metallique, outside hinge, $2,000-$2,500.

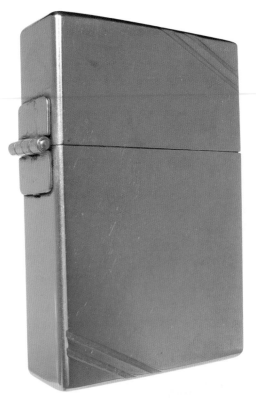

An early 1936 Zippo with outside hinge, $1,500-$1,800.

A 1936-37 lighter, Metallique, Louis the 14th, four-barrel hinge, $1,500-$1,800.

The back side of the Louis the 14th lighter, with initials.

Zippo lighters have been used as an advertising medium since 1935. What began as a company's way to promote its name and/or services has evolved into an avenue to promote practically anything.

Zippo lighters can be found bearing artwork depicting a variety of special events, people, places and things. Some of these Zippo lighters may spark a memory in you.

While many folks choose to collect whatever tickles their fancy, some folks focus on a particular theme.

Here, we have divided advertising into three sections: Companies, Events, and People, Places and Things.

Advertising—Companies

In this section, you'll find company advertising Zippo lighters, which advertise company names and services. These lighters are commonly referred to as "advertisers."

*A 1946 Zippo, Call for Philip Morris, Metallique, three-barrel, **$8,000+**.*

WHK Co., 1947, $125-$150.

Yale, 1947, $175-$200.

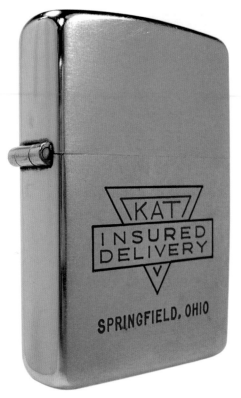

Kat, Insured Delivery, Springfield, Ohio, 1948, $125-$150.

Kist Beverages, Citrus Products Co., Chicago-U.S.A., 1951, $200-$250.

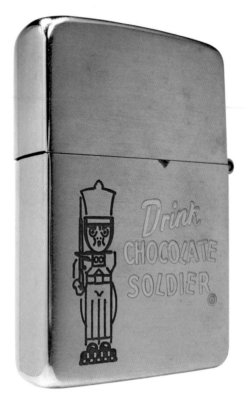

The back of the Kist Beverages lighter, Drink Chocolate Soldier.

Smith-Moore Body Co. Inc., 1951, $125-$150.

Cover the Earth, 1951, $150-$175.

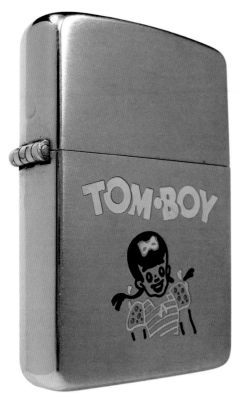

Tom-Boy, 1951, $150-$175.

Akers, 1952, $150-$175.

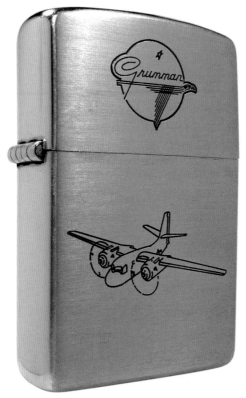

Grumman, 1952, $150-$175.

WAKR TV, Channel 49, 1952, $150-$175.

All, For Automatic Washers, 1953, $275-$300.

Good Beer, Griesedieck Bros. Brewery Co., St. Louis, MO, 1953, $175-$200.

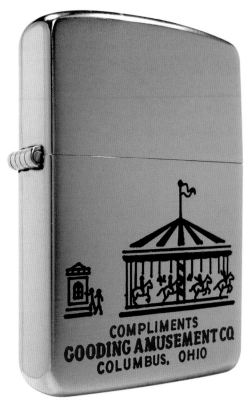

Gooding Amusement Co., Columbus, Ohio, 1953, $150-$175.

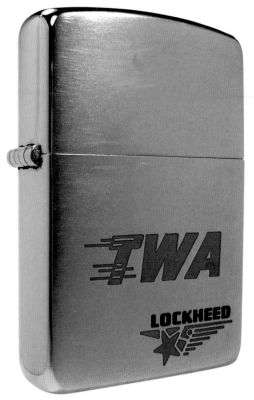

TWA, Lockheed, 1953, $150-$175.

Warman's Zippo Lighter Field Guide

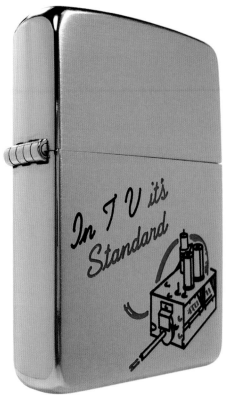

In TV it's Standard, 1955, $150-$175.

Raytheon Electron Tubes,
1955, $175-$200.

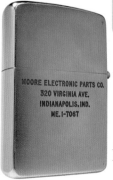

Back side of Raytheon lighter, Moore
Electronic Parts Co., Indianapolis, Ind.

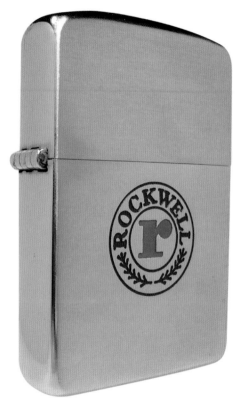

Rockwell, 1955, $125-$150.

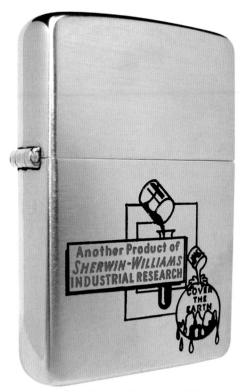

Another Product of Sherwin-Williams Industrial Research,
*1955, **$125-$150**.*

GE Refrigerators, 1956, $175-$200.

Aunt Jemima, 1956, $400-$450.

Good Humor Ice Cream Co., Season 1956, 1956, $175-$200.

Friden, 1957, $200-$225.

The back side of the Friden lighter.

State of Maine Products, Bangor & Aroostook Railroad, 1957, $200-$225.

Bill's Road Oiling Service, 1957, $100-$125.

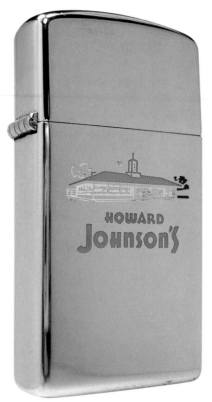

Howard Johnson's, slim, 1958, $250-$275.

The back side of the Howard Johnson's lighter, Motor Lodges.

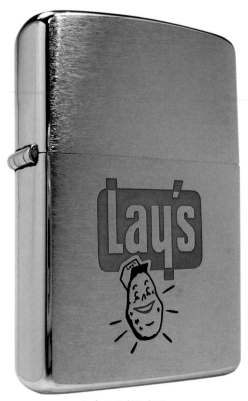

Lay's, 1958, $225-$250.

Permacel-LePage's Inc., 1958, $225-$250.

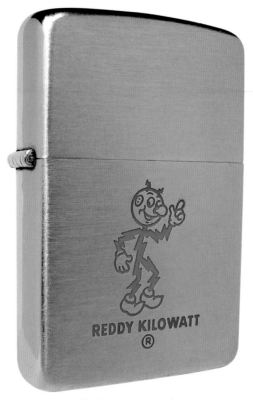

Reddy Kilowatt, 1958, $175-$200.

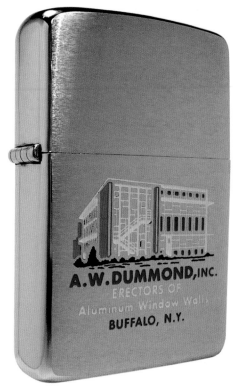

A.W. Dummond, Inc., Erectors of Aluminum Window Walls, Buffalo, NY, 1959, $125-$150.

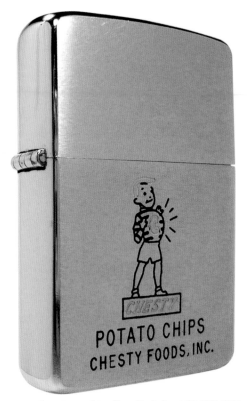

Chesty Potato Chips, Chesty Foods, Inc., 1959, $150-$175.

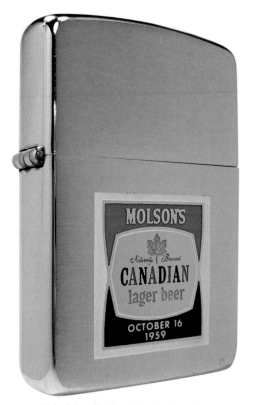

Molson's Canadian Lager Beer, 1959, $175-$200.

The Indiana National Bank of Indianapolis, 1959, $150-$175.

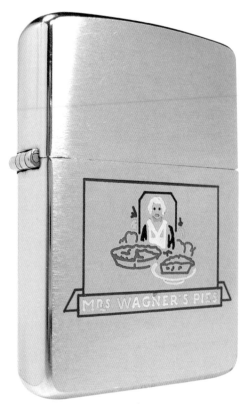

Mrs. Wagner's Pies, 1959, $225-$250.

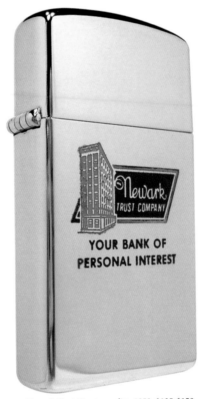

Newark Trust Company, slim, 1959, $125-$150.

The Regina Corp., Rahway NJ, 1959, $150-$175.

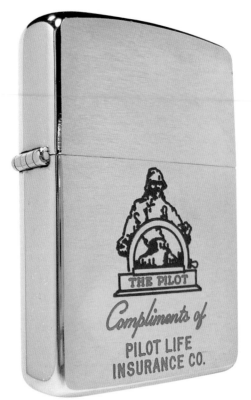

Compliments of Pilot Life Insurance Co., 1959, $100-$125.

Valvoline, The World's First Motor Oil, 1959, $175-$200.

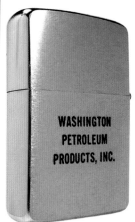

Back side, Washington Petroleum Products Inc.

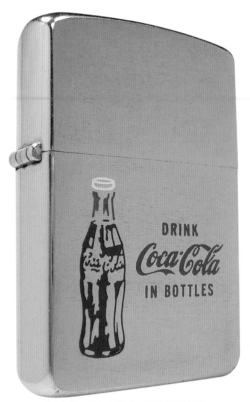

Drink Coca Cola in Bottles, 1960, $225-$250.

Warman's Zippo Lighter Field Guide

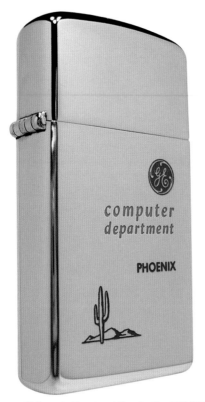

GE Computer Department Phoenix, slim, 1960, $90-$100.

*Gulf Aviation Products,
1960, $175-$200.*

*Back side,
Westchester County Airport.*

Warman's Zippo Lighter Field Guide

Singer Sewing Machine, 1851, Over a Century of Service, slim, 1960, $100-$125.

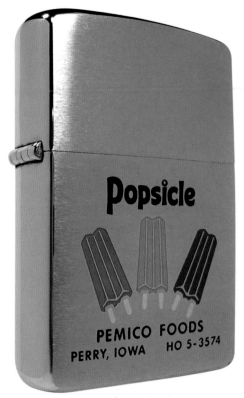

Popsicle, 1961, $500-$600.

Shakespeare, 1962, $175-$200.

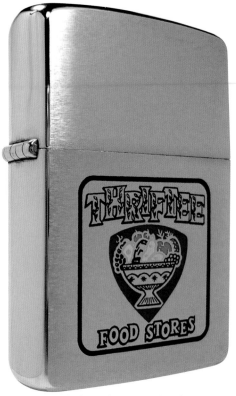

Thriftee Food Stores, 1962, $150-$175.

*Planters, Mr. Peanut,
The Name for
Quality, slim, 1963,*
$325-$350.

Sinclair Oil & Gas Company,
1963, $325-$350.

Back side, Sinclair
Truflame LP Gas.

Top Value Stamps, 1963, $125-$150.

Cream of Wheat Cereal, 1964, $275-$300.

Eastern Overall Cleaning Co. of Easton, Easton, PA, 1964, $150-$175.

Dutch Boy Paints, 1965, $225-$250.

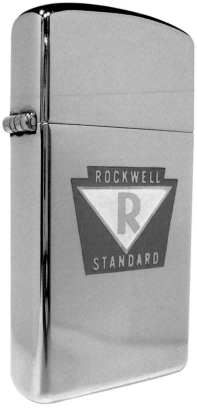

Rockwell Standard, slim, 1965, $75-$100.

Anheuser, 1966, $100-$125.

Lowe Brothers Paints, slim, 1966, **$125-$150**.

G. R. Myers Motor Transportation, Barberton, Ohio, 1966, $100-$125.

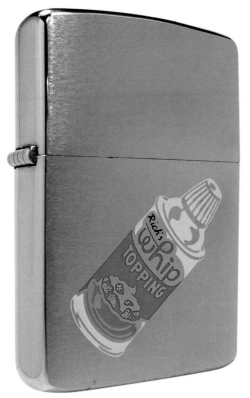

Rich's Whip Topping, 1966, $225-$250.

Stanly Knitting Mills, Inc., Oakboro, NC, Ladies' Hosiery, slim, 1966, $125-$150.

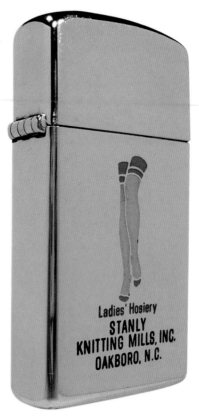

The back side of Stanly Knitting Mills, Inc., Ladies' Full Fashioned Sweaters.

Sunkist, 1966, $275-$300.

Texaco, slim, 1966, $75-$100.

D&G, 1967,
$100-$125.

Red felt insert, which was used primarily in the mid-1960s.

Compliments of Hage Funeral Home, Charles City, Iowa, 1967, $75-$100.

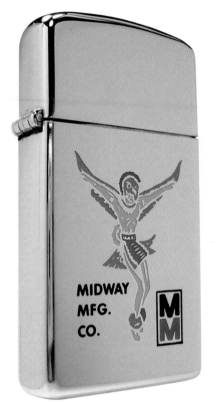

Midway Mfg. Co., slim, 1967, $100-$125.

Hertz, slim, 1968, $500-$550.

Hertz, open.

Beeline Fashions, slim, 1969, $100-$125.

Byerly Mobile Homes, Kirkwood, Missouri, 1969, $100-$125.

Corn King, Ham & Bacon, 1969, $100-$125.

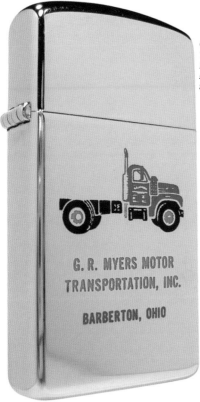

G. R. Myers Motor Transportation, Barberton, Ohio, slim, 1969, $75-$100.

Pohl Tool Co., Detroit 4, Mich., 1969, $75-$100.

Sherwin-Williams Paint, 1969, applied emblem, $75-$100.

Arctic Cat, Farmers Cooperative, Thorp, Wis., 1970, $175-$200.

The Chase Manhattan Bank, N.A., slim, applied emblem 1970, $100-$125.

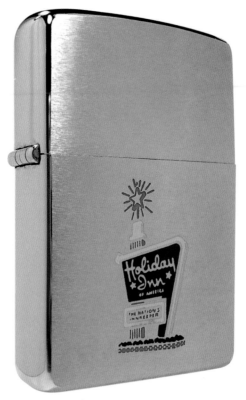

Holiday Inn, 1970, $225-$250.

Ruttman Mini-Bikes, 1970, $125-$150.

Back side, Dearborn Heights, MI.

A Reddy Kilowatt slim, 1971, $125-$150.

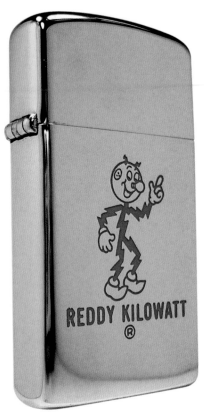

UniCan, Shrewsbury, Mass-Long Beach, Cal., 1971, lossproof, $100-$125.

Duncan Industries, Division of Qonaar Corp., slim, 1972, $75-$100.

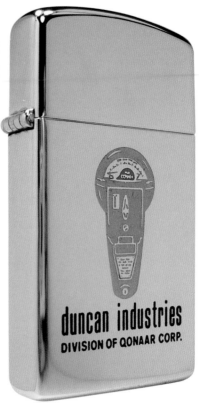

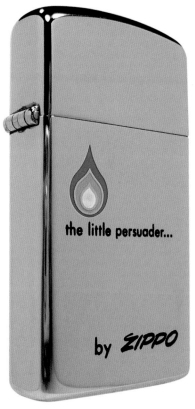

The little persuader, slim, 1972, $125-$150.

Parkhill, Joplin, Missouri, slim, 1972, $75-$100.

The back side of the Parkhill lighter.

Pittsburgh Paints, 1972, $325-$350.

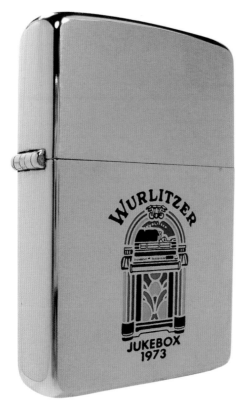

Wurlitzer Jukebox, 1973, 1972, $175-$200.

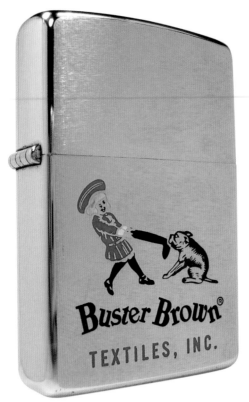

Buster Brown Textiles Inc., 1973, $250-$275.

Clark Equipment Automotive Division, Buchanan, Mich, slim, 1973, $75-$100.

Back side of lighter.

*ITT Arctic Services,
slim, 1973,
$100-$125.*

Rich's Coffee Rich,
slim, 1973,
$100-$125.

Sherwin-Williams Paint, slim, 1973, $50-$75.

UniCan, slim, 1973, $50-$60.

Wes-Tex Drilling Company, slim, 1973, $75-$100.

Pittsburgh Paints,
slim, 1974,
$275-$300.

Eastern Kentucky Mack, Inc., slim, 1974, $100-$125.

Back side of Eastern Kentucky Mack lighter.

Stag Beer, 1974, $75-$100.

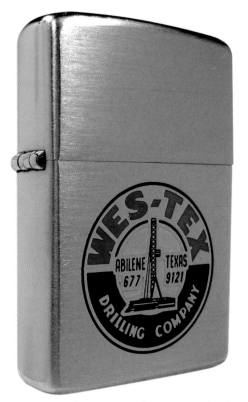

Wes-Tex Drilling Company, Abilene, Texas, 1974, $100-$125.

Boeing, 1975, $125-$150.

Campbell's Soup, 1975, $275-$300.

Piper Cherokee 140, 1975, $125-$150.

Purina Kitten Chow, 1975, $75-$100.

Benjamin Moore Paints, Southwestern Paint & Wallpaper Co., Houston, Texas, slim, 1976, $50-$75.

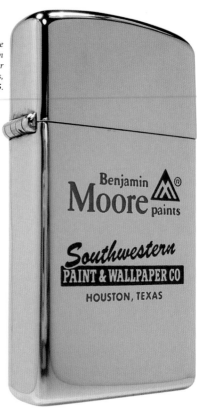

Marlboro, 1976, $100-$125.

Harley Davidson, 1976; first Harley Davidson advertiser offered for sale to the public, slim, $75-$100. Ron Chapin's personal Harley Davidson advertisers can be seen here: http://home.mchsi. com/~abaldguy/

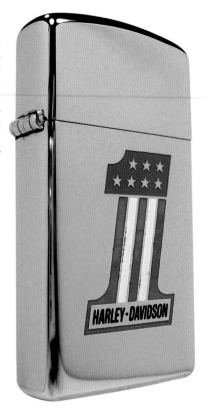

Chevrolet, There's No Match for Step-Van, slim, 1976, **$75-$100**.

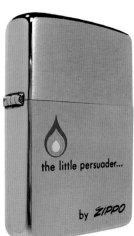

The little persuader...by Zippo, 1976, **$150-$175**.

*Dutch Boy Paints,
slim, 1977,
$200-$225.*

*Enjoy Coca Cola, slim, 1977, **$125-$150**.*

Back side of lighter, written in Greek.

Swiss Miss, 1977, $200-$225.

Fischer's, the Bacon-makin' people, 1978, $100-$125.

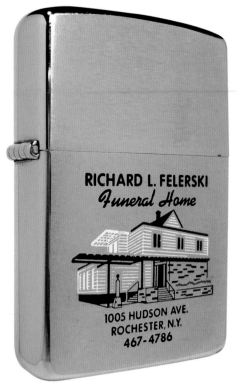

Richard L. Felerski Funeral Home, Rochester, NY, 1978, $175-$200.

Heinz, slim, 1980,
$200-$250.

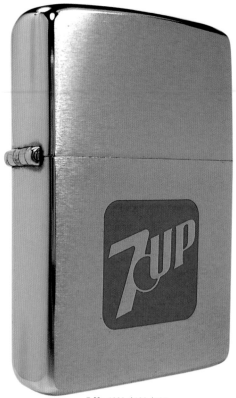

7-Up, 1980, $100-$125.

7-Up, slim, 1980,
$75-$100.

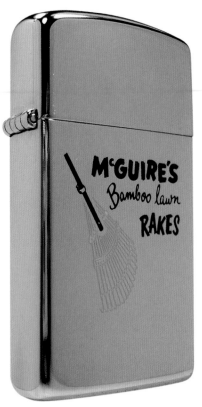

McGuire's Bamboo Lawn Rakes, slim, 1980, $100-$125.

*Louisiana Inland Schlumberger,
slim, 1981, $75-$100.*

Back side of the lighter.

Havoline Texaco,
slim, 1985,
$30-$35.

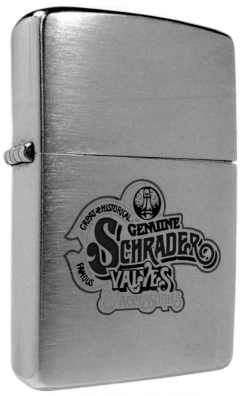

Genuine Schrader Valves, 1985, $75-$100.

*Harley Davidson,
slim, 1987,
$50-$60.*

Mack Trucks, 1988, $100-$125.

Mack Trucks, slim, 1988, $75-$100.

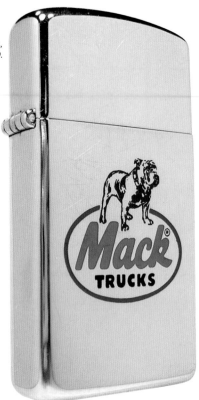

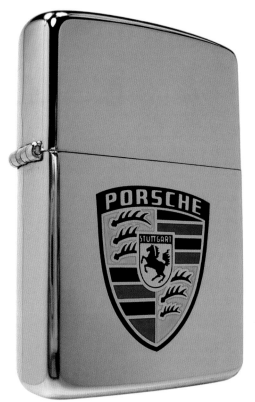

Porsche, 1988, $50-$75.

Harley Davidson Motor Cycles, 1989, $40-$45.

Midnight Chrome Classic Camel, 1992, no initials, $50-$75.

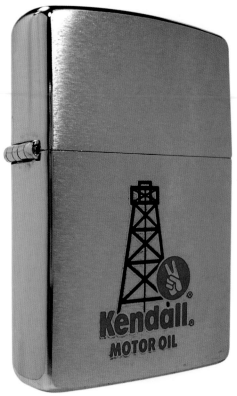

Kendall Motor Oil, 1992, $50-$60.

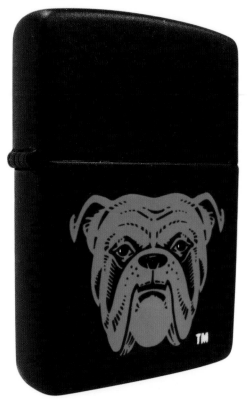

Red Dog, 1994, $25-$30.

Camel, antiqued brass biker emblem, 1995, $90-$100.

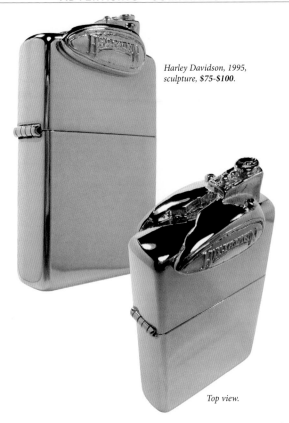

Harley Davidson, 1995, sculpture, $75-$100.

Top view.

Camel Pop Art, 1996, $125-$135.

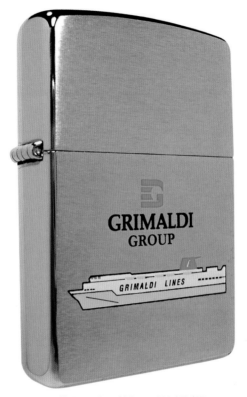

Grimaldi Group, Grimaldi Lines, 1996, $50-$55.

Miller High Life, 1996, $55-$60.

Playboy, 1996, $30-$35.

Bud Ice, 1997, $30-$35.

Harley Davidson Worldwide, 1997, $45-$50.

House Blend Uniquely Aromatic, 1997, $30-$35.

Tabasco Pepper Sauce, 1997, $35-$40.

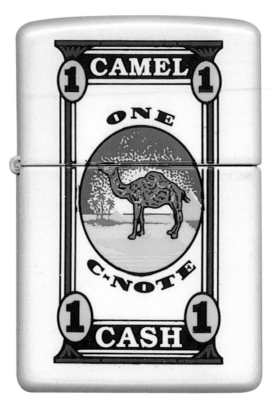

Camel C-Note, two-sided, 1998, $150-$175.

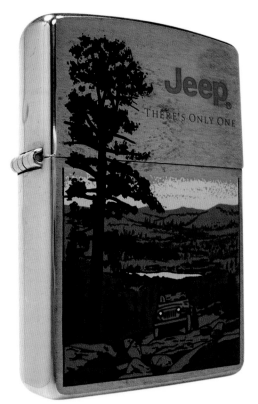

Jeep, There's Only One, 1998, $35-$40.

*Playboy,
slim, 1998,
$25-$30.*

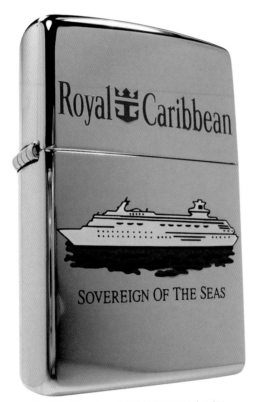

Royal Caribbean, Sovereign of the Seas, 1998, $65-$75.

Tropicana, 1998, $150-$175.

Winston Filter Cigarettes, 1998, $200-$225.

Miller Genuine Draft, 1999, $35-$40.

Pleasurable Piercings Inc., 1999, $30-$35.

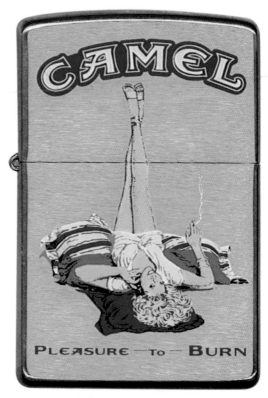

Camel, Pleasure to Burn, 2000, $150-$160.

Marlboro, Moon Over Mountains, 2000, $20-$25.

Harley Davidson Motor Cycles, 2000, side mount, $45-$50.

Another view of the Harley Davidson lighter.

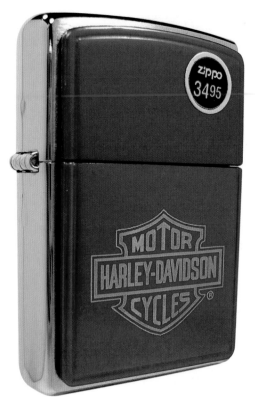

Harley Davidson Motor Cycles, 2001; retail: $34.95.

Lufthansa, Airbus A340-300, 2001, $70-$80.

Playboy, 2003; retail: $32.95.

Santa Fe Natural Tobacco Company, 2003, $35-$40.

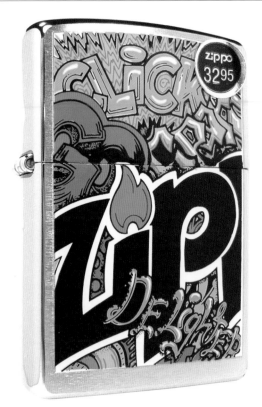

"Graffiti" by Zippo, 2004; retail: **$32.95**.

Roseart, Gifts of Lifetime Elegance Since 1957, Bradford, PA, 2004, (limited to 75), $50-$60.

Advertising—Events

In this section, you'll find Zippo lighters produced in recognition of important world events, various anniversaries, festivals, awards, and holidays.

United Airlines, Commemorating Inaugural Flight City of Bradford, 1948, $275-$300.

Back side of lighter.

Ice Capades, 1951, $300-$325.

Duo-Therm 25th Anniversary 1927-1952, 1952, $150-$175.

Stewarts Private Blend Coffee, 40th Anniversary, 1953, $150-$175.

Ellis, One Year Without Accident, 1954, $125-$150.

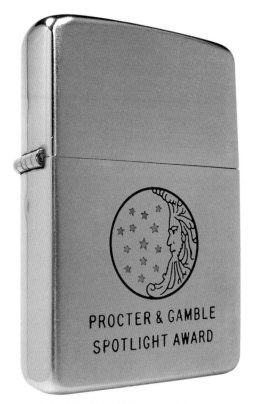

Procter & Gamble Spotlight Award, 1957, $150-$175.

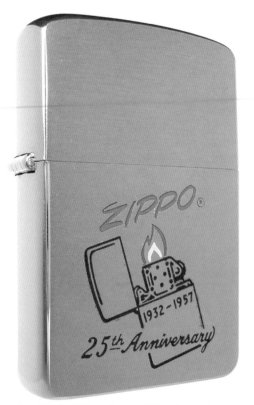

Zippo 1932-1957 25th Anniversary, 1957, single panel, **$550-$600**.

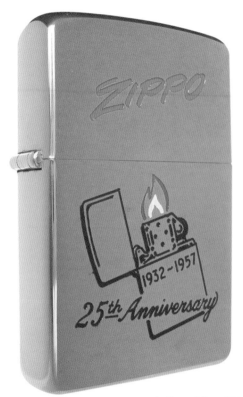

Zippo 1932-1957 25th Anniversary, 1957, double panel, $650-$700.

*Andy Griffith Show,
Fourth Great Year, slim,
1963, $250-$275.*

*Back side of lighter, We
Appreciate It-Sanka Coffee.*

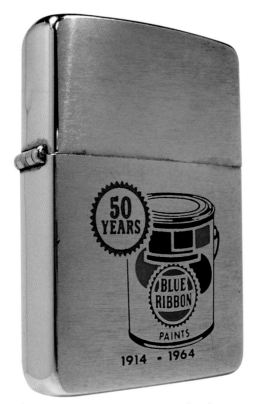

Blue Ribbon Paints, 1914-1964 50 Years, 1963, $150-$175.

*Ford Steel Division
5th Safety Award,
Blast Furnaces
1,000,000 hours
April 1963, slim,
1963, $100-$125.*

General Pencil Co., Jersey City, NJ, 75th Anniversary 1889-1964, slim, 1964, $125-$150.

American Steamship Co. Safety Award, 1964 Sailing Season, 1964, $100-$125.

Metropolitan Transit CTA Suggestion Plan 25th Anniversary,
1969, $75-$100.

Baby Ruth, 50th Anniversary, slim, 1971, $100-$125.

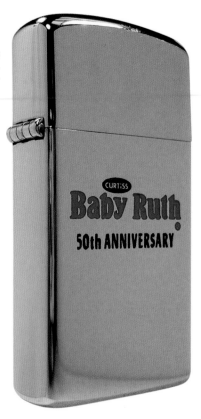

Zippo's 40th anniversary, 1972, $50-$75.

Budweiser, Michelob, Busch, slim, 1976, $125-$150.

Back side, American Bicentennial, 1776-1976.

Bicentennial, 1976, $100-$125.

*Bicentennial,
slim, 1976,
$75-$100.*

Copperweld Steel Company, I Am a Think Ideas Winner, 1976, $50-$75.

Look Alive with Lees, America's Favorite Carpet Leadership Conference 1976, 1976, $50-$75.

Zippo Plant Visitation, April 1979, Bradford, PA, slim, 1978, $200-$225.

Kentucky Derby, 1980,
$125-$150.

Back side of lighter.

Bus Bash 1981, Olean, NY, Hosted by Blue Bird Coach Lines, slim, 1981, $75-$100.

Zippo's 50th Anniversary, 1982, $50-$75.

*Kinzua Bridge, Mt. Jewett Pennsylvania, 1882-1982, 100th Anniversary,
1982, $75-$100.*

Camel, 75th Birthday, Camel 75 years and Still Smokin', 1988, $225-$250.

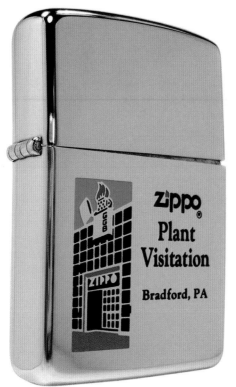

Zippo Plant Visitation, April 1979, Bradford, PA, regular size, 1988, $200-$225.

*Case, 1889-1989 100th Anniversary, slim, 1989, $75-**100**.*

Warman's Zippo Lighter Field Guide

Big Boy, Over 50 Years (limited edition of 500), slim, 1991, $100-125.

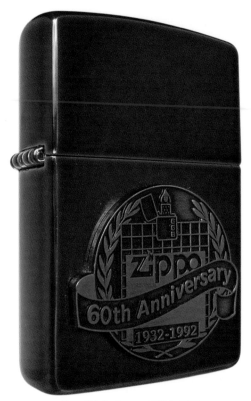

Zippo 60th Anniversary, 1992, $50-$75.

Merry Christmas, 1994, $50-$60.

Babe Ruth, 100th Anniversary, $75-$100.

Camel, Season's Greetings from the Camel Family, 1997, $125-$130.

Atlanta 1996 Olympic Games, 1996, $40-$45.

Zippo-South Africa 15th Anniversary, 1982-1997, B.L. Agencies, 1997, (50 produced), $100-$125.

95 Harley Davidson Years, 1903-1998, 1997, (4,000 produced), $100-$125.

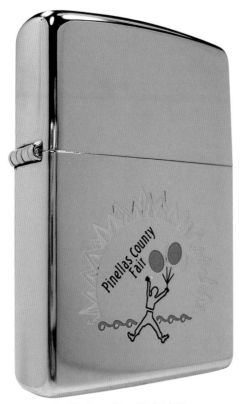

Pinellas County Fair, 1997, $75-$100.

Bradford High School, Class of 1948 50th Reunion, 1998, $75-$100.

*Duke of Zuke, 1998,
$75-$100.*

*Back side, 2nd Annual
Zucchini Festival, Ludlow,
Vermont, August 1998.*

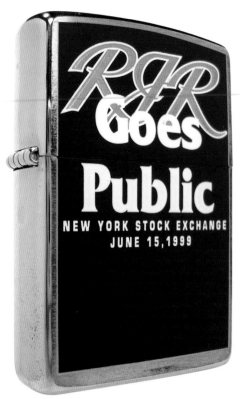

RJR Goes Public, New York Stock Exchange, June 15, 1999, 1999, $75-$100.

Playboy's 45th Anniversary, $50-$75.

Biker Tour 2000, 2000, $150-$175.

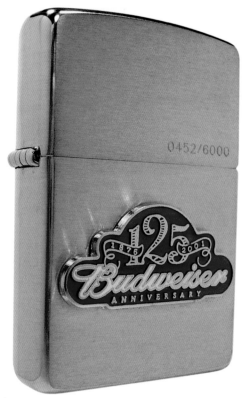

*Budweiser, 1876-2001 125th Anniversary (6,000 produced), 2001, **$50-$75**.*

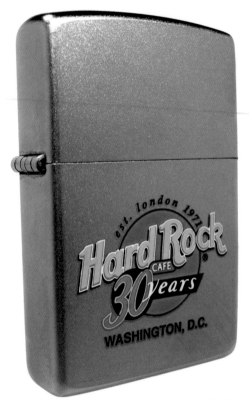

Hard Rock Café, est. London 1971, 30 Years, 2001, $50-$60.

Thanksgiving, 2001; retail: $22.95.

Zippo South Africa,
1982-2002
20th Anniversary, 2002,
$50-$60.

Zippo's 70th Anniversary,
2002, $75-$100.

Easter theme, 2003;
retail: $31.95.

OTLS 20th Anniversary (three produced),
2003, value undetermined.

Advertising—
People, Places and Things

In this section, you'll find Zippo lighters with artwork representing people, clubs and fraternal organizations; places from around the world including casinos, famous landmarks, and restaurants (known as "souvenir" lighters); and even a game and a movie.

Golden Nugget, Las Vegas, Nevada, 1946, $350-$400.

Member, Ohio Funeral Directors Ass'n, Inc., 1947, $150-$175.

Masons, 1947, applied emblem, $125-$150.

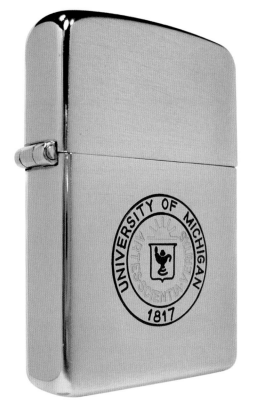

University of Michigan 1817, 1947, $150-$175.

Kiwanis International, 1949, applied emblem, $125-$150.

Baker Aircraft Sales, Municipal Airports, Long Beach and San Jose California, 1955, $175-$200.

Blue Mountain Skeet & Trap Club, 1955, $150-$175.

Moslem Temple Detroit, Marvin G. Lane Potentate, 1955, $100-$125.

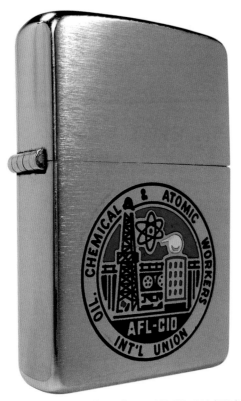

Oil, Chemical & Atomic Workers Int'l Union, AFL-CIO, 1956, $200-$225.

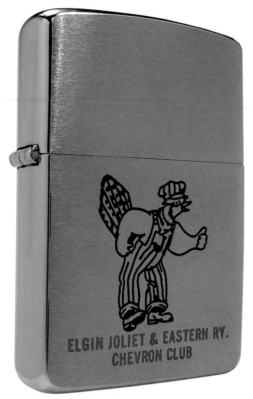

Elgin Joliet & Eastern RY Chevron Club, 1959, $150-$175.

Tradewind Airport, Amarillo, Texas, 1961, **$125-$150***.*

Mother of Perpetual Help, 1963, $125-$150.

Barry Goldwater, slim, 1964, $75-$100.

Inter American Press Association, slim, 1964, $50-$75.

The Westerner Club, 1969, $50-$60.

Monterey Motel Restaurant, Best Western Motels, Mexico, MO, 1971, $150-$175.

Yellowstone National Park, 1972, $125-$150.

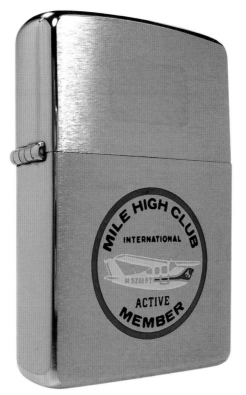

*Mile High Club, International Active Member, 1976, **$125-$150**.*

Ringling Bros. and Barnum & Bailey, Circus World, slim, 1976, $175-$200.

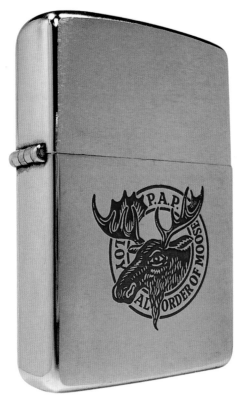

P.A.P. Loyal Order of Moose, 1978, $50-$75.

Sonic, Happy Eating, Hamburgers, Onion Rings, slim, 1978, $100-$125.

Six Flags Great Adventure, 1979, $50-$75.

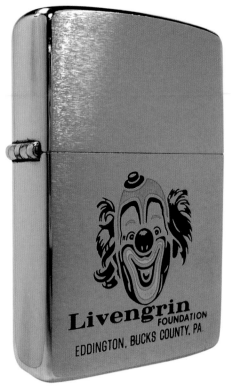

Livengrin Foundation, Eddington Bucks County, PA, 1983, $125-$150.

Elvis Presley, slim, 1987, $50-$75.

Chicago Fire Department, 1989, $30-$35.

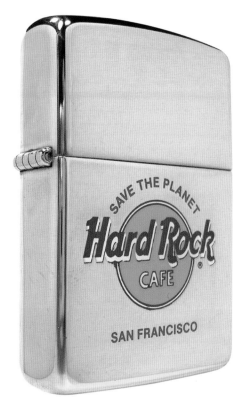

Hard Rock Café, Save the Planet, San Francisco, 1989, $35-$40.

George Bush/Mikhail Gorbachev, 1990, $40-$50.

Mt. McKinley, Alaska, 1991, $35-$40.

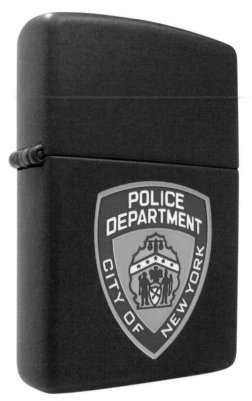

City of New York Police Department, 1991, $30-$35.

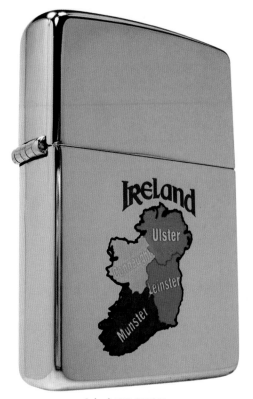

Ireland, 1993, $35-$45.

University of Miami, slim, 1993, $60-$70.

American Legion, 1994, $25-$35.

Winston Churchill, 1994, (less than 75 exist), $75-$100.

Stargate, Eye of Ra, 1994, $30-$35.

Niagara Falls Skyline, 1995, $45-$50.

Experience New York, 1996, $50-$75.

Mother of Perpetual Help, slim, 1996, $50-$75.

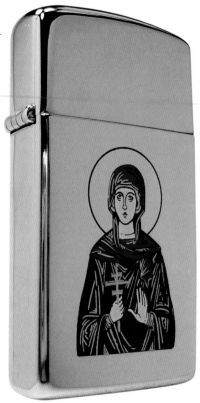

Sloppy Joe's, Hemingway's Favorite, Key West, 1996, $30-$35.

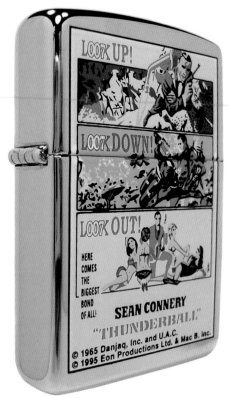

007 Thunderball, 1996, $45-$50.

Camel, Pool League, 1997, $250-$275.

Harrahs, Atlantic City, 1997, $35-$40.

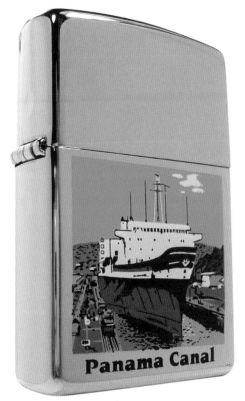

Panama Canal, 1997, $35-$40.

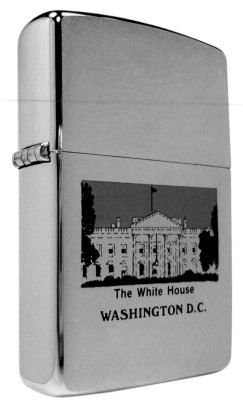

The White House, Washington, D.C., 1997, $45-$50.

Lighter Club of Great Britain, 1998 Convention, 1998, $60-$75.

Ellis Island, 1998, $35-$40.

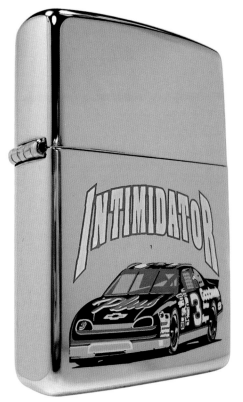

Intimidator, 1998, $35-$40.

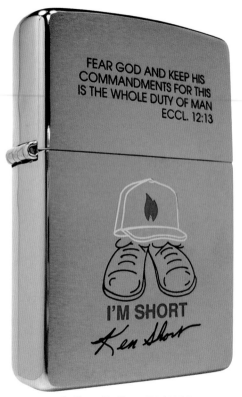

I'm Short...Ken Short, 1998, $50-$60.

Zippo, Ski Slope, 1998, $35-$40.

Circus Circus, Las Vegas, 1999, $35-$40.

KISS, 1999, $25-$30.

Mirage, Las Vegas, 1999, $35-$40.

Vienna, 1999, $35-$40.

BB King, New York, rose gold finish, slim, 2000, $45-$50.

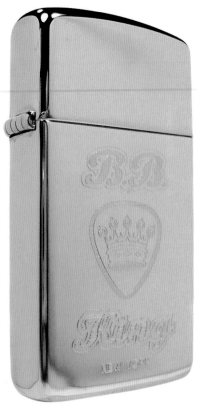

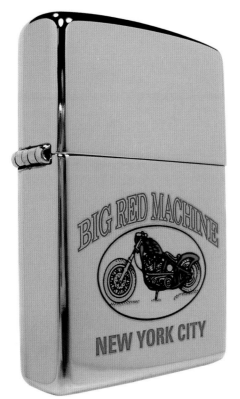

Big Red Machine, New York City, 2000, $35-$40.

Hard Rock Hotel, Las Vegas, 2000, $40-$45.

Hooters, York, PA, $35-$40.

Harley Davidson Café, Las Vegas, 2001, $30-$35.

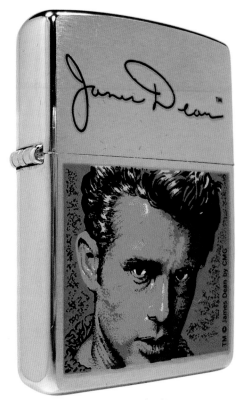

James Dean, 2001, $30-$35.

Zippo Collectors Club, Holland, 2002, $40-$45.

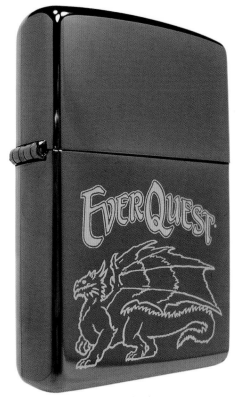

Everquest, 2002, $25-$30.

In Loving Memory, Wally Laird, 1933-2002, 2002, $50-$60.

Images of America, Zippo Manufacturing Company, 2003, $35-$40.

Big Ben, 2004, $30-$35.

Warman's Zippo Lighter Field Guide

Caesars, 2004, $30-$35.

Zippo Club, Austria, 2004, $35-$40.

Pennhills Country Club, Bradford, PA, 2004, 50 produced, $45-$50.

Back side of lighter, individually numbered.

Adam Johnson, Works Like a Tiger on the Zippo Team, 2004, $30-$35.

TOWN AND COUNTRY

The Town and Country process was introduced in the late 1940s using a paint-on-paint labor-intensive method. The designs were deeply engraved onto the case and then paint was applied using an airbrush.

The original series included geese, horse, lily pond, mallard, pheasant, setter, sloop, and trout. Lighters decorated with the Town and Country process having no paint loss are highly regarded by collectors and often afford high prices. Town and Countrys first retailed for $7.50. The last official Town and Country was the commemorative done for the 1969 moon landing.

The Shreveport Times, 1958, $150-$175.

The Shreveport Times, 1970, slim, transitional T&C, $175-$100.

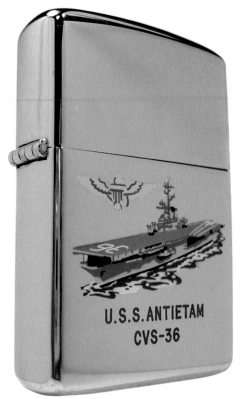

USS Antietam, CVS-36, 1958, $175-$200.

Rooster,
slim, 1960,
$400-$500.

USS Greenwich Bay AVP-41, Commander U.S. Middle East Force, 1960, $175-$200.

William Scott Mach. Co. Inc., Detroit, Michigan, slim, loss proof, 1961, $500-$550.

B & L Motor Freight Inc., Newark, Ohio, 1964, $325-$350.

Rip Van Winkle Lanes, Norwalk, Conn., slim, 1965, $325-$350.

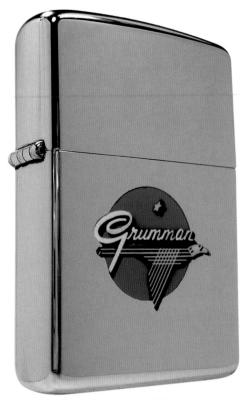

Grumman, 1966, $325-$350.

Leather-crafted lighters came in several variations, as this Zippo ad shows.

Full leather, green,
$400-$500.

Bottom
marking of
full leather.

Full leather, black,
$400-$500.

Brown alligator wrap, $300-$400.

Red leather wrap, $300-$400.

Zippo lighters have played an important role in every war since World War II. They warmed hands, started campfires, provided light, and even deflected bullets. Zippo lighters became constant companions for the troops and were small reminders of what they left behind. Commonly referred to as "trench art," some servicemen used their Zippo lighters as a drawing board to reflect their feelings and they would decorate their lighter cases with hand-etched designs.

Because of a shortage of brass, all Zippo lighters during WW II were made of steel and dipped in black paint and then baked. This produced what is known as a "black

Black crackle, $350-$400.

crackle" finish. It is said this process was to prevent rust and to cover up the uneven surface that was evident in the production of the steel case. GIs liked it because it was non-reflective. During WW II, all Zippo lighters manufactured were shipped to PXs for our military's use. During the Korean War, again due to the shortage of brass, the cases were made of steel. Production of chrome-plated brass lighters resumed at the end of both wars.

All branches of the Armed Services have been represented on Zippo lighters at one time or another. Zippo Manufacturing Company has produced several commemorative lighters honoring those who have served and commemorating various military milestones.

Rolf Gerster maintains an informative Web site of military Zippo lighters at www.gersters.ch.

Korea Zippo lighter of Lieutenant Colonel William W. Cox, 2nd Medical Battalion, 1951, $200.

Back side of Lt. Col. Cox's lighter.

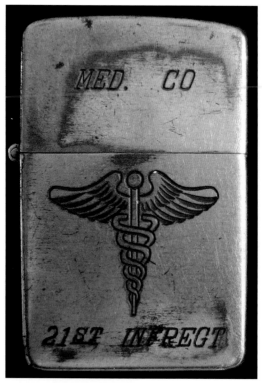

Korea Zippo lighter of Paul Howard, Medical Company, 21st Infantry Regiment, 1951, $150.

Back side of Howard's lighter.

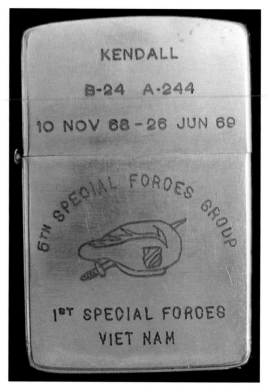

Zippo lighter of Sergeant Timothy J Kendall, U.S. Army Special Forces, Teams B-24/A-244, 1968, $350.

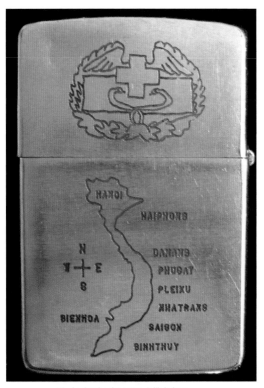

The back side of Sgt. Kendall's lighter.

Zippo lighter of 1st Lieutenant Loren H Flicker, 8th Field Hospital, 1966, $220.

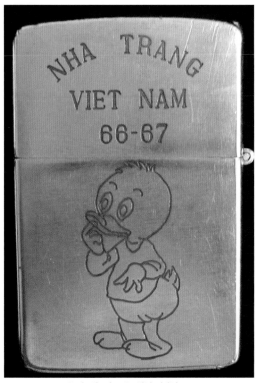

Back side of 1st Lt. Flicker's lighter.

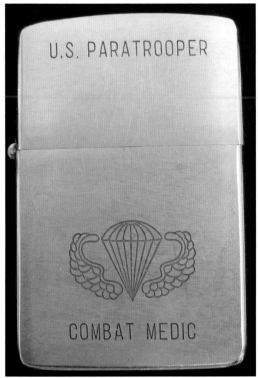

*Zippo lighter of Combat Medic Guevara, 2nd Battalion, 505th Infantry Regiment (Airborne Infantry), 1968, **$200**.*

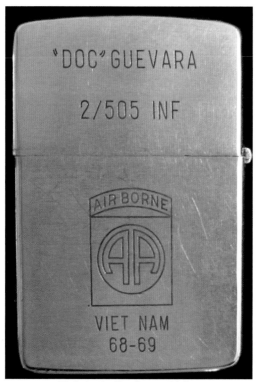

The back side of "Doc" Guevara's lighter.

*161st Aviation Company, 1967, **$300**.*

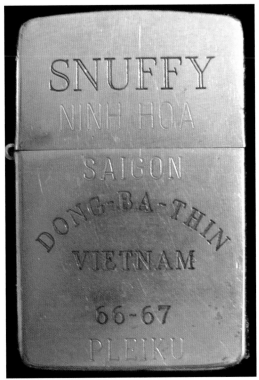

*Zippo lighter of Snuffy, 1965, **$100**.*

The back side of Snuffy's lighter.

Warman's Zippo Lighter Field Guide

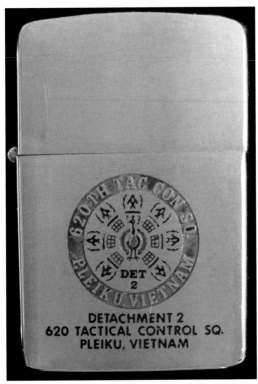

620th Tactical Control Squadron, Detachment 2, Pleiku, 1968, $300.

18th Special Operations Squadron, 1971, **$150.**

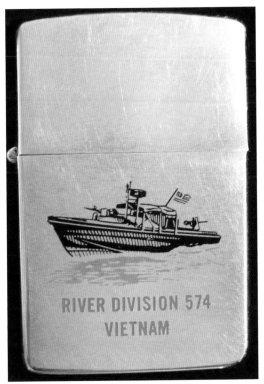

River Division 574, 1969, $350.

The back side of the River Division 574 lighter.

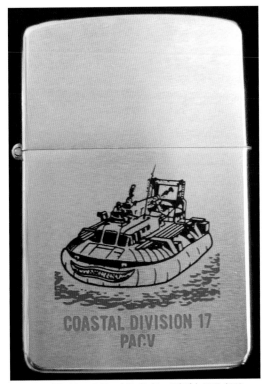

*Coastal Division 17 (Patrol Air Cushion Vehicle), 1969, **$350**.*

Zippo lighter of Petty Officer 2nd Class George L. Sparks (Steel Worker Fabricator, Seabees), 1962, $180.

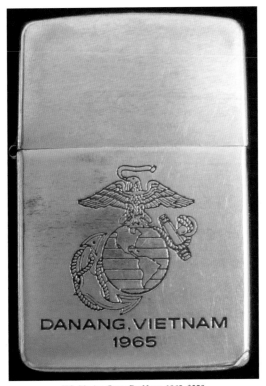

U.S. Marine Corps Da Nang, 1965, $250.

*Zippo lighter of J. M. Rottman, 1st Marine Division (USS Sanctuary AH-17), 1966, **$180.***

Back side of lighter.

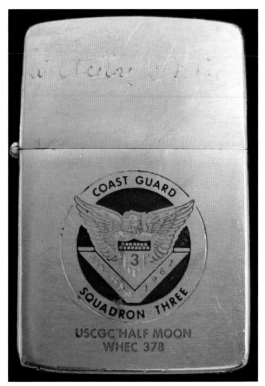

U.S. Coast Guard Cutter Half Moon WHEC 378 (Coast Guard Squadron Three), 1967, $350.

Commander Coastal Squadron Three, 1970, $300.

American Embassy in Saigon, 1969, **$250***.*

Fourth Battalion Royal Australian Regiment (Australia - New Zealand Army Corps), 1969, $200.

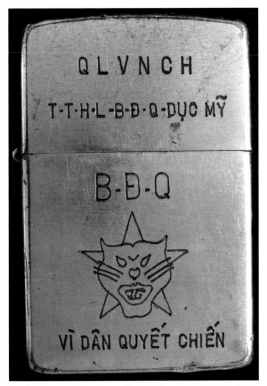

South Vietnamese Army Ranger Training Center Duc My, 1972, $150.

Korean unit in Vietnam, 1966, $250.

The back side of the Korean lighter.

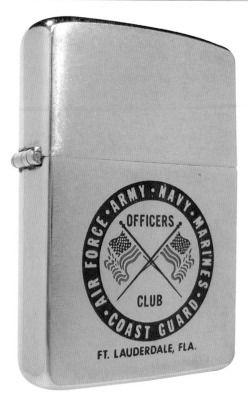

Air Force, Army, Navy, Marines, Coast Guard Officers Club, Fort Lauderdale, Fla, 1957, $125-$150.

*South Vietnamese 23rd Infantry Division, Ban Me Thuot (U.S. advisor Staff Sergeant Robert Lindman), 1967, **$350**.*

*Hanchin, Thai Police, 1969, **$100**.*

The back side of the lighter.

USS Belleau Wood LHA-3, slim, 1993, $50-$75.

Naval Air Station, Pensacola, Florida, 2000, $50-$75.

SPORTS

Undoubtedly, the earliest and longest lasting series produced is the sports series. Here we'll show you a small example of its progression. We have not included every lighter produced for every period. You will see some pieces with the optional "lossproof" feature though. Lossproof Zippo lighters, introduced in 1947, have a metal loop attached through the lighter's hinge enabling a lanyard to be drawn through it. Lighters with the lossproof feature have additional value. The lossproof model is still available today.

In 1937, "line drawn" designs were etched into the surface of the case and filled with enamel paint, and 17 different patterns were available.

In the early 1950s, the designs were filled with a variety of colors.

In 1958, commonly referred to as "two panel" or "double panel," designs done on the lid and bottom of the case were popularized.

The sports models of 1981-1983 were produced using only three or four colors.

A circle of color was the background of the sports series produced beginning in 1982. Here you will see some examples of the paint variations between lighters painted in the U.S. and Canada, which we discussed earlier.

A spectacular burst of design and coloring was brought about in 1997. A new series patterned from the 1997 series was released in 2002.

Zippo has also produced scores of other sports-related lighters and series.

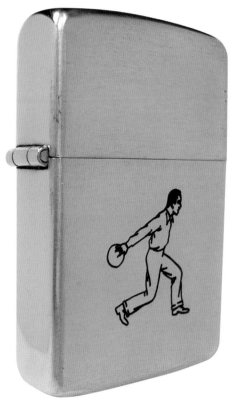

Bowler, 1946, $200-$300.

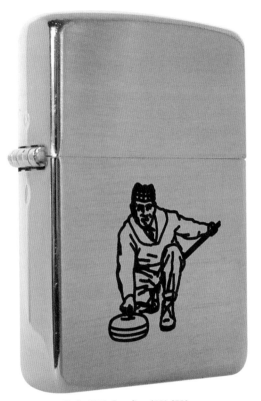

Curler, 1949, Canadian, $500-$550.

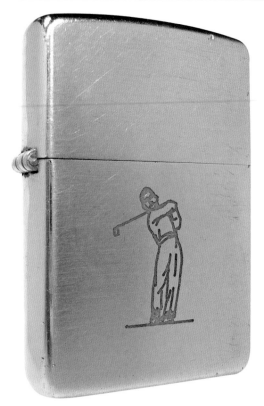

*Golfer, 1949-51, **$150-$175**, if in excellent condition.*

Golfer, 1953, $150-$175.

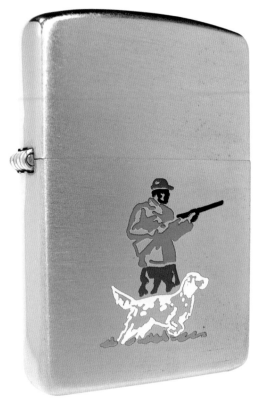

Hunter, 1953, $175-$200.

Baseball, 1954-55, lossproof, $425-$475.

Bowler, 1956, $150-$175.

Fisherman, 1956, $175-$200.

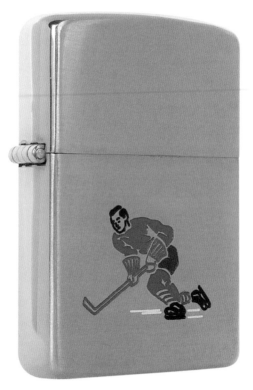

Hockey player, 1957-59, Canadian, $250-$275.

Bowler, 1958, short-sleeved, $200-$225.

*Bowler, 1958,
slim, $300-$325.*

Fisherman, 1958, lossproof, $275-$300.

Curler, 1959, Canadian, $375-$400.

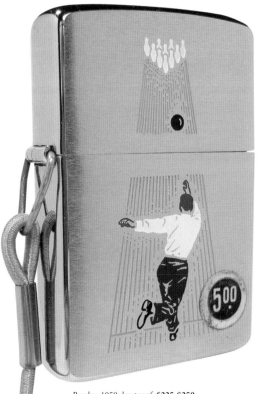

Bowler, 1959, lossproof, $225-$250.

*Bowler, slim,
1964,
$250-$275.*

Golfer, 1962, $100-$125.

Skier, 1965, $250-$275.

Fisherman, 1968, $100-$125.

Bowler, early 1970s, Canadian, $125-$150.

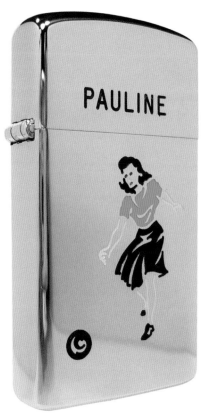

PAULINE

*Bowler, 1971,
Pauline,
$250-$275.*

Snowmobiler, 1970, $200-$225.

Fisherman, 1971, $75-$100.

Golfer, 1972, $65-$75.

Snowmobiler, early 1970s, Canadian, $125-$150.

Snowmobiler, 1974, $75-$100.

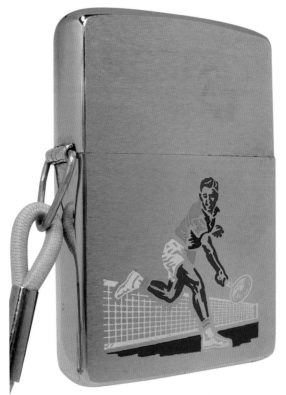

Tennis player, 1980, lossproof, $60-$75.

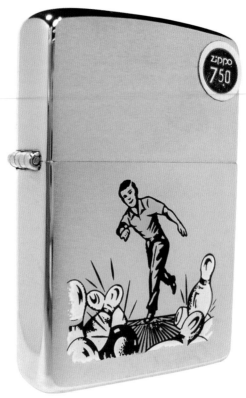

Bowler, 1981, $75-$100.

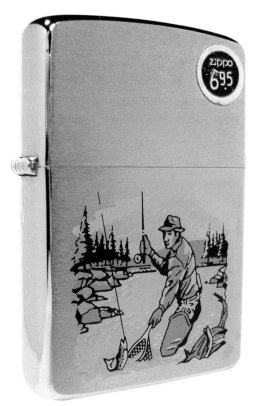

Fisherman, 1981, $75-$100.

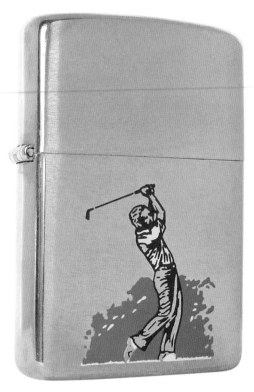

Golfer, 1981, $30-$40.

Skier, 1981, $125-$150.

Hunter, 1982, $100-$125.

Fisherman, 1984, $20-$25.

Baseball, 1989, Canadian, $60-$65.

Bowler, 1991, $20-$25.

Bowler, 1992, Canadian, $25-$30.

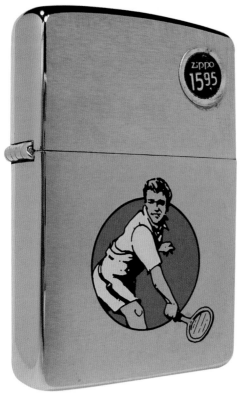

Tennis player, 1993, $20-$25.

Hockey player, 1994, Canadian, $55-$60.

Dart player, 1995, $45-$50.

Hunter, 1995, $20-$25.

Pool player, 1995, $50-$55.

Baseball, 1997; retail: $25.95.

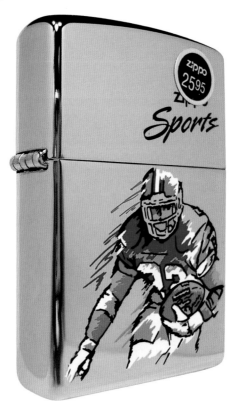

*Football, 1997; retail: **$25.95**.*

Golfer, 2000; retail: $27.95.

Hunter, 2000; retail: $27.95.

NFL display panel.

Saints, slim, 1971, $75-$100.

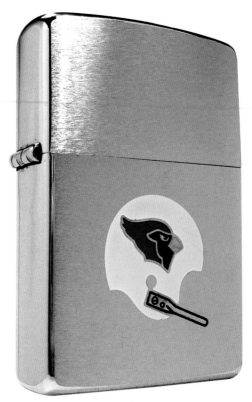

Cardinals, 1972, $100-$125.

*Miami
Dolphins, slim,
1973,
$75-$100.*

NFL, 1974, $100-$125.

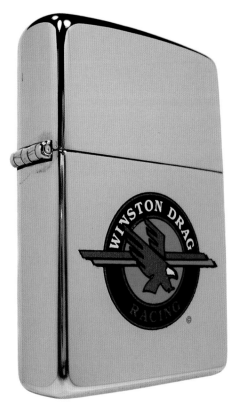

Winston Drag Racing, 1994, $40-$50.

Broncos, 2000, applied emblem, $35-$40.

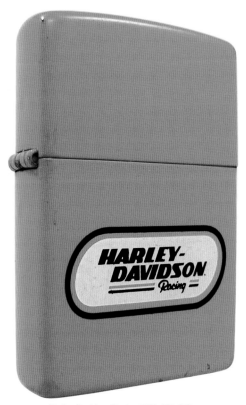

Harley Davidson Racing, 2000, $35-$40.

Zippo began production of its first table lighters ("Barcroft" lighters) in 1938-39. They retailed for $7.50 and were produced until 1940-1941. This model was 4-1/2 inches tall and is referred to as a "One Step" or "1st Model," which has one step at its base.

In 1947, the model was reintroduced, and the case was shortened to 4-1/4 inches, the "2nd Model," which has two steps.

The lighter was shortened again in 1949-1950 to 3-1/4 inches, which became the "3rd Model." These first three models had large inserts.

The large insert was replaced with the smaller insert, used in regular size Zippo lighters we see today, in 1953-1954, the "4th Model." Production was discontinued circa 1979.

Lady Bradford—This model began in 1949 and was discontinued in the early 1950s (see P. 434).

Roseart—Roseart, also located in Bradford, teamed up with Zippo and began production in 1957. Roseart products are still produced today. Visit www.roseartlighters.com for more information (see P. 435).

Moderne—Introduced in 1960, the Moderne was available in black, bright rhodium and satin rhodium finishes and retailed for $12.50. Production was halted in 1966 (see P. 437).

Corinthian—Like the Moderne, this model ran from 1960 until 1966 and retailed at $16.50. It was available in chrome, pearlescent, and turquoise finishes (see P. 438).

Handilites—This line started in 1979 and was discontinued at the end of 2002 (see P. 439).

Lady Barbara—The Lady Barbara was introduced in 1997 as part of Zippo's 65th anniversary. Lady Barbaras were added to the product line in 1998 and discontinued at year end 2002 (see P. 443).

Barcrofts

Personalized "The Wiley's," 2nd model, $150-$200.

Shakertown Sidewalls Cleveland Ohio, 3rd model, $250-$300.

*Good Year Racing Tires, 4th model, **$150-$175**.*

Airstream, 4th model, $150-$175.

Mickey Mouse, 4th model, $800-$900.

Kool, Flip-Open Box, 4th model, $200-$250.

Russo Around the Clock Answer-Phone Service, 4th model, $200-$225.

Sonic, 4th model, $225-$250.

*Westinghouse (vending machine),
4th model, $600-$700.*

*Back side, Automatic
Merchandising Springfield
Massachusetts.*

Lady Bradford

Lady Bradford, 1950, $175-$200.

Roseart

*Roseart, 1958, **$350-$375**.*

*Roseart, black and gold Italian marble, 2003; retail: **$199.95**.*

*Roseart, cherry, slim, 2004; retail: **$97.95**.*

Moderne

Moderne, $125-$150.

Corinthian

*Corinthian, turquoise finish, **$150-$175.***
*Chrome finish is **$125-$150.***

Handilites

*American Airlines, 1979, **$125-$150**.*

*Pepsi, 1979, ultralite, **$200-$225**.*

Lynn Hickey Dodge Inc.,
Oklahoma City, OK, 1995,
$150-$175.

Back side, Cowboy Coupe.

Super Steelers, Super Bowl IX, X, XIII and XIV Champions, 1979, $150-$175.

Plain brass, 1998, $50-$60.

SCRIMSHAWS

Scrimshaw lighters were first test marketed in 1976 and early 1977 using true scrimshaw. It was very costly, so true scrimshaw was replaced with acrylic. The scrimshaw series remains available today.

Outrigger, 1977, $650-$750.

A sales sheet for the Scrimshaw collection.

Ship, 1984, $30-$35.

Ship, black matte, 1990, $30-$35.

Whale, red matte, slim, 1997, $35-$40.

Ultralites were launched in 1978. The black onyx is still available today.

Black Onyx, 1978, $30-$40.

ZIPPO ULTRALITES

The sales sheet for Ultralites.

Hawaii, 1978, ivory, $50-$60.

OSU Go Bucks, slim, 1981, $40-$45.

Masters, slim, 1983, $40-$45.

Indianapolis Hoosier Dome, 1984, $60-$75.

Barcelona '92, slim, 1989, $60-$75.

Contempos were a line of butane lighters Zippo had produced in Japan under license throughout the 1980s.

Tortoise standard, $55-$65.

Contempo

**NEW Butane Collection
by ZIPPO**

It's exciting! It's elegant! It's
contemporary! It's Zippo's entry into
the butane lighter market and it's
called Contempo. Zippo has been
manufacturing lighters for over 50
years and its fine reputation for expert
craftsmanship combined with today's
sophisticated styling and technology
are bound to make Contempo a
best-seller. Contempo is quality in
the Zippo tradition . . . quality you can
pass on to your customers with pride.

A - Style #712, Gold Mesh Standard $39.95
B - Style #1412, Gold Mesh Trim $39.95
C - Style #1413, Burnished Gold Trim $39.95
D - Style #713, Burnished Gold Std. $39.95
E - Style #1415, Basic Black Trim $59.95
F - Style #715, Basic Black Std. $59.95
G - Style #1411, Louver Gold Trim $29.95
H - Style #711, Louver Gold Std. $39.95
I - Style #703, Louver Chrome Std. $39.95
J - Style #1403, Louver Chrome Trim $29.95
K - Style #1416, Tortoise Trim $29.95
L - Style #716, Tortoise Std. $59.95
M - Style #714, Burgundy Std. $59.95
N - Style #1414, Burgundy Trim $59.95
O - Style #1401, Bright Chrome Trim $29.95
P - Style #701, Bright Chrome Std. $29.95
Q - Style #702, Fluted Chrome Std. $29.95
R - Style #1402, Fluted Chrome Trim $29.95

ZIPPO MANUFACTURING COMPANY · BRADFORD, PENNSYLVANIA 16701/IN CANADA - ZIPPO. MFG. CO. OF CANADA LTD., NIAGARA FALLS, ONTARIO
86-35-C5S   Printed in U.S.A.

The sales sheet for Contempo Zippo lighters.

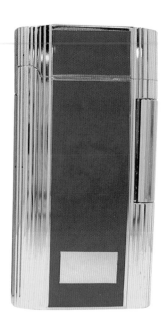

Burgundy, slim, **$50-$60;** *standard,* **$60-$70.**

Bright Chrome, slim, $40-$50; standard, $50-$60.

Zippo Manufacturing Company came out with "Collectible of the Year" Zippo lighters in 1992 and introduced a new Collectible of the Year for the next 10 years.

1992, Zippo 60th anniversary pewter emblem on midnight chrome finish; retail: $19.95.

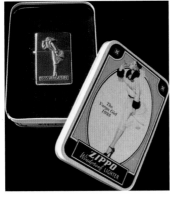

1993, Windy; retail: $19.95.

*1994, D-Day, retail: **$24.95**. Shown with companion four-lighter set, Allied Heroes, retail: **$82.75**.*

*1995, Mysteries of the Forest four-lighter set; retail: **$109.95**. Shown with companion Jaguar and Cub at Turtle Falls; retail: **$27.95**.*

*1996, Zippo Salutes Pinup Girls; retail: **$29.95**. Shown with Four Seasons companion set; retail: **$119.95**.*

1997, Zippo 65th anniversary; retail: $32.95.

*1998, Zippo Car and keyring; retail: **$32.95**.*

1999, One World One Future, millennium-themed titanium lighter;
retail: $26.95.

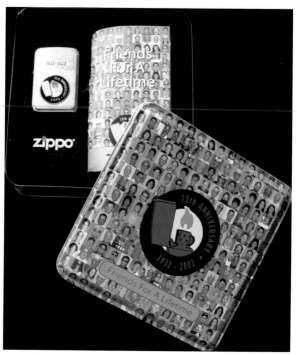

2002, Friends for a Lifetime commemorating Zippo's 70th anniversary, limited to 70,000 pieces; retail: $39.95.

Zippo, keeping with the times, produced some groovy lighters for the '70s. The company continues that marketing strategy of producing attractive, up-to-date designs, which appeal to a large and varied audience, to this day. Examples shown here represent a tiny fraction of lighter series/designs done by Zippo.

While all Zippo lighters are manufactured in Bradford, PA, some of them are shipped to Japan for decorating. Once there, Zippo's Japanese distributors, under license, may decorate Zippo lighters with artwork and techniques approved by Zippo. Several Japanese-issued lighters are available on-line. One place we recommend you try is www.zippostation.co.jp.

Also under license, Claudio Mazzi, an airbrush artist residing in Italy, creates one-of-a-kind, limited series, and open series, using Zippo lighters as miniature canvases for his paintings. His "Zippo By Mazzi" lighters are available for sale at the Zippo/Case Visitors Center and through distributors around the world. Mr. Mazzi's official Web site is www.zippobymazzi.it.

Peace sign, slim, 1970, $100-$125.

Smiley face, 1971, $125-$150.

Smiley face, slim, 1971, $100-$125.

Zodiac series, Virgo, slim, 1974, one of 12, $125-$150.

Denim display panel.

Cat, denim, 1975, $75-$100.

Mickey Mouse, denim, slim, 1979, $350-$375.

Warman's Zippo Lighter Field Guide

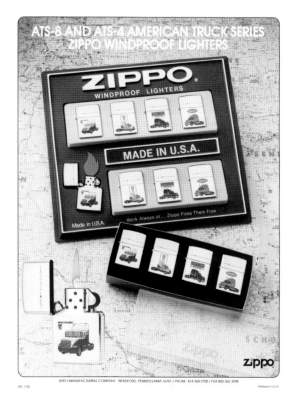

A sales sheet for the American Truck Series, 1992.

*Peterbilt, 1992, one of four pieces, **$40-$45 each***.

Blue Angels display panel, 1993.

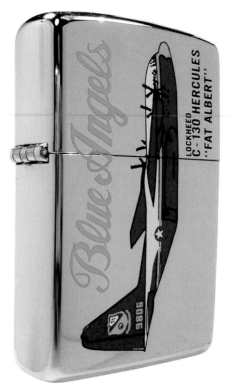

Lockheed, C-130 Hercules "Fat Albert," 1993, one of eight pieces,
$40-$45 each.

Six-piece Harley Davidson puzzle set, 1997, ***$175-$200.***

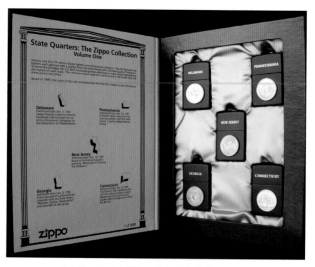

State Quarters Set, Volume 1, 1999, limited to 5,000 sets,
$150-$175.

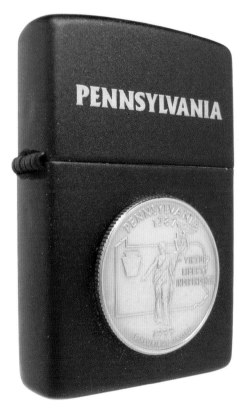

The Pennsylvania lighter from the State Quarters set.

*Space Explorations, A Remembrance, Volume III, 1999,
limited to 10,000 sets, $150-$175.*

The Space Shuttle lighter from the Space Explorations set.

Surprise lighter, 1999, $30-$40.

EGYPTIAN KING

This design was taken from the actual Death Mask found when Howard Carter opened the coffin containing King Tutankhamen's mummy. On his helmet are the traditional symbols of upper (The Vulture) and lower (The Cobra) Egypt.
Above the mask is a widely used stylized Papyrus motif.

Like the timeless treasures of the Egyptian tombs, your Zippo lighter will last a lifetime.

Treasure of the Tomb Series, Egyptian King, 2000; retail: $34.95.

Carson Waterman-Reflections, 2002, one of four pieces;
retail: $25.95-$29.95 each.

Babes collection, 2002;
retail: $42.95.

Back side.

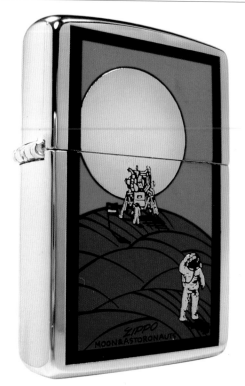

While all Zippo lighters are manufactured in Bradford, the one here, as well as the ones on pages 497 and 498, were decorated in Japan. Moon and Astronauts, 1994, $100-$125.

Changes of Zippo Fuel Containers, silver-plated, 2003, $50-$75.

Changes of Zippo Fuel Containers, silver-plated, 2003, $50-$75.

Also under license is artist Claudio Mazzi, who designed this lighter, as well as the ones on pages 500 and 501. Zippo by Mazzi, one of a kind, painted in 2003 on a 1947 lighter, $500-$600.